When Perseverance Opportunity

A True Story About A Small Business that
Went International on The Wings of Angels

And how a hobby-turned to business and the
business kept me rolling in dough.

Special Edition

Advance Reader Copies 11-25-2017
Publishing Date 1-1-2018

By Carol A. Graziano

www.Bootstrappublishing.net
Leaving Legacy Program
mkd@bootstrappublishing.net
585.342.0795
480.560.4933

The creator of Kneeded Angels™
Rochester artist

Published in the United States of America

Adoughables
by
Carol A. Graziano

"... waiting to share
their gentle beauty with you."

Dedication

P roudly and without hesitation, I dedicate this book to my two sons, Jamie and Patrick Graziano. Being a stay at home Mom was a wonderful experience. When we became a threesome, I had to find a "Real job." Always working on my hobby, I also found a full-time position. Many hardships emotionally and economically with their support and family and friends we made it through. Today I am truly proud of my sons who are successful business men.

Christmas Angel 2017

I gave them life, they gave me joy.
At the sum of my life I dedicate this book to the both of you.
I love you, I love you more. Smile "143."

And to my grandchildren, Kayleigh and Alec Graziano have been the love and joy of my life since the moment they were born. I used to think *"I don't babysit, I have play days with them."*.

We would play restaurant fun with them. I would be the patron with my dog, Alec played the Maître-Dei. He would seat me at my reserved table. With a towel over his arm he became the connoisseur of soda, lemonade or tea. Kayleigh became the lovely waitress as she handed me the menu. Minutes later with pad and pen in hand to take my order.

Christmas Eve was another extra fun time. One of us started a story and each of us would add to it. I miss those days when they would both run to me, I would think, oh *gosh, how can I pick them up at the same time.* Today they are adults with independent lives.

And to
My friend Carole Hall, a true artist,
Thank you, and may you rest in Creativity Peace.
Love you More.

My Life's Vision

I want to be that someone, that through my figurines and angels, brings a smile and a forgotten memory, as they do for me. I was told by my publisher to write about ten of my angels. It was an awesome experience.

"When I finished, I realized I was telling my life story through my angels."

Before creating from my own vision, I would purchase many Hallmark greeting cards and coloring books for ideas. I would focus on children, their outfits and style of their hair, such as pigtails or braids. I would think "I can make that child in dough." If you just think about it, we are all surrounded by beautiful things and people.

It's like being a human scanner until suddenly something or someone truly stands out in my mind.

So, what do you get when you mix imagination, perseverance, sandwich bread, and Elmer's Glue?

Read On.

My Life's Mission

"It all started out to" make someone smile today."
I even used to tell my kids before they left the house for school,
"make someone smile today."

My Name is Carol Graziano,
this is my story of how a hobby-turned business and the business
kept me rolling in dough.

That Gut Feeling

If or when you get that
gut feeling
that you have
something to offer,
wrap your faith around it.
Believe me, your dreams,
your goals will become
bigger than you can ever imagine.
Your dreams and goals at times may wither,
but that's only because your faith has withered.
Something will remind you, wake you up,
and then "Boom" you start getting that faith back
and you're on the road again.
When a situation arises because it seems you are changing
your dreams and goals, that is o.k. You will always grow into them.
That perseverance, meeting up with opportunity will come and
flourish and become bigger than you have ever imagined.

Love and Luck Carol

The Story in A Nutshell
Foreword

Introduction

What do you get when you mix imagination, perseverance, sandwich bread, and glue?

ADOUGHABLES

She goes through more than 1,300 loaves of sliced white sandwich bread and 60 gallons of glue a year. No, she's not on some weird diet, but "glue dough" has become her recipe for success. What has become her life's work started when her sons were young and in Cub Scouts, and she found a recipe for baker's clay. "I started making frogs, ants, and worms for my sons and the Scouts," she said with a laugh. Then when she took the items to her first "show," the church bazaar at St. Margaret Mary's Church, she said she was surprised they were selling. "Adoughables by Carol," Graziano creates original, handcrafted, porcelain-like figurines from what may seem a strange concoction. Her designs and creations run the gamut from wedding cake tops and Nativity scenes to Santa Clauses, clowns and dolls. Her collections are exhibited in arts and crafts shows throughout Monroe County and western New York, and her collectible line of doll figurines known as "Sunday's Best" has been gaining her notoriety nationwide. The process of creating these detailed figures is a lengthy one, but one she refers to as a labor of love. Sitting in Graziano's home, you can see that she loves her work. A photo album of the bridal cake tops she has made through the years is among her works. The figurines bare a striking, uncanny resemblance to photos of the real brides and grooms. Graziano said that she spends hours creating them in likeness of the couple, right down to the sequins on a dress and the flowers in a bouquet.

She points to little pink jogging shoes delicately dangling from a bridal bouquet to illustrate her point. Each creation is taken to heart, and Graziano goes to great lengths to make sure her Adoughables are true-to-life.

"I've even went to the florist to see what the bouquet looked like and to the dress shops to see the back of the bridal gown that you can't see in a photo," she added. She said many couples have brought their cake tops back after a few years to have her add a baby or two to round out the family – a request she fulfills willingly. Each of Graziano's "Sunday Best" line – Maggie, Jillie, Rebecca, and Ebony – is different, from the dresses they wear to the bows in their hair. Most have **her trademark blue eyes.** Although her business today is riding high with marked success, Graziano says it didn't start out that way.

The Webster native began working in the dough medium as a hobby in 1973, a time when she says she had no artistic talent at all. Soon her repertoire was expanded to include caterpillars and Santa Clauses. She later began exhibiting in small arts and craft shows and church bazaars, but her perseverance didn't stop there.

"It's been my escape," she said. *"I find nothing more relaxing." "They are an extension of myself,"* Graziano said. *"These kids become my kids, my babies."* There are times Graziano will create a figure and not be able to part with it upon completion. She prefers to make each of her collectibles individually, since mass production would take away from her creativity.

"I'm finally doing what I love to do, that is a recipe for success in the world of Adoughables."

Adoughbles to The Kneeded Angels™

Out of the great mixing bowl of life came the Kneeded Angel's.

Each Kneeded Angel is creatively kneaded, rolled and wrapped to become a one of a kind masterpiece. They are all handmade from a very special dough-like material. The originals, created by Carol Graziano, use the same technique, however are made with bread and glue. The Kneeded Angels are accompanied by an inspirational recipe card.

It was the Park Avenue Festival in 2001 that has made the biggest difference in her life. It was at that festival that Graziano was approached by Zina and Rich Hocker, owners of Pavilion Gift Co. in Bergen, N.Y. "They told her that she did the cake topper for a cousin's wedding and they wanted to know what sells the most," Graziano recalled. She was quick to respond, "angels!"

They had a meeting a week later *"and my life has become a whirlwind of creativity, joy, and emotional bliss ever since,"* Graziano said. The company not only asked Graziano to come up with 22 contemporary designs by Oct. 15 that year, and introduced her to a manufacturer in Toronto.

Graziano's designs were sent to the Orient for reproduction. Twenty-two of Graziano's angel designs, in addition to her 11-piece nativity set hit the gift show market across the country in January. Her line has 14 pages in the newest Pavilion Gift catalog.

The first "Kneeded Angels," as the reproductions are called, began arriving in gift shops across the county in late May of that year. They're already available in more than 2,000 shops in the U.S. and Canada, including Hallmark stores and Army and Navy base gift shops. Some of the stores have already sold out and are doing reorders. Among the most popular designs to date is a patriotic angel holding a flag.

While Graziano has been making her creations for more than 25 years, she says now, "Gosh, I feel like I have won an Oscar... I have!"

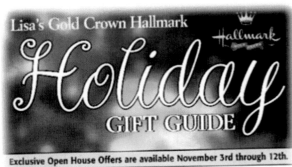

Her dream has always been to have her work on display in a shop, she said, but she has never had the inventory to fulfill that dream.

"My mass production is six," she said. Now, she can continue making her originals, which she will be selling at arts and craft shows locally, while at the same time being able to see the reproductions in gift shops.

Graziano is already in demand to sign her reproduced work, and her first signing in Rochester was at Village Gifts in Fairport. She was also at Lock, Stock and Barrel in Eastview Mall, Oliver's Candies in Pittsford and at County Cabin Gifts in Webster, where she grew up.

"It's all coming together," Graziano said. *"I wish I could visit every shop they're in and have a picture of me and the display!"* **All from humble beginnings.**

Graziano has called Irondequoit her home for over 50 years and raised her two sons, Jamie and Patrick, both graduates of Irondequoit High School.

She kept striving to improve and combed greeting cards and coloring books for ideas. Then she found the glue and sandwich bread recipe, which she has fine-tuned over the years, and started making pins, then dolls. She liked the new material because all it needed was to be air-dried. The crust is ground separately for use as teddy bears or robes.

One night a week, on Thursday, four friends, including Rosenbauer, all of whom she met as customers, come over for a "fancy" dinner at Graziano's house and to help with some of the basic work.

Rosenbauer and Graziano go back more than 20 years. "That part is so rewarding because the brides and their families are so appreciative," Graziano said, adding she loves talking with her customers. "Tell me this isn't the most rewarding business to be in," she said. "I still get emotional after all these years. All of the people I meet are so beautiful."

If you asked many business students how to start a business, make millions of dollars in annual sales, employ 70 people in upstate New York and operate manufacturing plants in China, the response might not lay out a plan to make angels and inspirational figurines. Yet that is what Zina and Rich Hocker have done in Bergen, Genesee County. And while the U.S. economy may be a bit sour, orders are keeping gift manufacturer Pavilion Gift Co. busy.

Rich Hocker said the company's sales have been great all year, and that October was the best shipping month in its 10-year history. "I think (the shipping numbers) surprised a lot of people. ... We feel very blessed to be in the situation we're in right now," said Zina Hocker. The company, which made its first retail shipments in October 1998, has 70 employees, including designers, artists, sales support staff, warehouse staff and accountants. Zina Hocker said Pavilion Gift is well-known for its line of inspirational collectible figurines, which once included the Zingle Berrys, now a retired line.

Current products lines included the Kneeded Angels, designed by Irondequoit artist Carol A. Graziano. Sales of the angels have exceeded 1 million units, said Hocker. Graziano said she has been working for Pavilion Gift for almost seven years. She said the Hockers have arranged signings at trade shows in Atlanta and the United Kingdom, each of which drew hundreds of admirers.

"It's been a Cinderella story," said Graziano. "The Hockers are people people. ... They're interested in what people are looking for." to having her designs sold at this time 3,000 stores worldwide has required plenty of problem-solving. In years of designing with dough, **the highs have outweighed the lows.**

They were sold at more than 900 Hallmark stores nationally and local gift shops in the Rochester area, including most hospital gift shops. Her Christmas tree ornaments are sold through Avon Canada. "How many people get to do what I do" marvels Graziano, whose early design included caterpillars. "It's all turned into a beautiful butterfly." Graziano's basement workshop is stocked with the same materials she started at the kitchen table: Elmer's glue and loaves of white bread, stored frozen. But now her basement counters, shelves and tables are covered with cups of paintbrushes, tubes of paint and glitter. Bald angels stand near Santa's. Measuring spoons hang from nails. Tiny dough hearts and paper flowers await use.

Graziano has learned much through trial and error. Each piece is made in stages, because the dough should harden – sped along by a fan – to hold the next part. For the range of skin tones, she settled for watercolors because they don't stain her hands.

After machine-mixing and hand-kneading the dough, it's softer than clay, more like silly putty. Graziano uses a cookie cutter to cut out an angel's robe. Sometimes she presses lines or design into the figure's clothing with a rubber stamp or textured fabric. She uses hard-to-find round toothpicks to create natural-looking sleeve folds.

Getting foreign workers to copy her techniques required more trial and error. In photos, early figurines look as if they had the mumps. A manufactured king looked like Yoda. Graziano made a one-hour step-by-step training video. Now workers mimic her designs except for the faces, which are applied in China with a decal of her signature eyes for consistency rather than hand-painted.

Graziano was the first artist with whom Rich and Zina Hocker worked after they started Pavilion. "She has the ability to put together products in a marketable way," says Rich Hocker, praising her energy, attitude and unique creations.

Mass production has allowed Graziano to expand and make a good living. When she made everything herself, she would make six of one design at a time, because doing more was boring. The most copies she ever made of one item was 200. except for her limited-edition angels, she makes only one of each contemporary design to be shipped overseas. She says it would be nice if her work could be mass-produced in this country, but the pieces wouldn't be affordable. "That's the bottom line. "Because she still likes to exhibit at about three craft shows a year – including the Holiday Bazaar at the Rochester Museum and Science Center – she buys back some of Pavilion's reproductions, removes the face decal, paints the features and makes other alterations by hand. She calls her local business Adoughables. Her prices range from $5 for a sheep to $80 for a Santa Claus.

Along the way, Graziano has learned from various failures. Home parties, à la Tupperware, didn't work because customers wanted everything customized. Being part of a craft cooperative and having a store didn't last. And her first contract with a big company was canceled because neither was satisfied.

The True Story About
A Small Business
Went International
On the Wings of Angels

Getting Started
Adoughables By Carol

Her Story in Her Words.

Five years of being a stay-at-home Mom, I found a recipe for bakers 'clay consisting of flour, salt and water. I made some ants on a log, worms and frogs. My sons, Jamie and Patrick were very young at the time and I thought they might enjoy them. I had no artistic ability at the time. My friend Carole Hall, a true artist, who went to college on an Art Scholarship, had a craft sale at her home. Wow! I sold them for $.50 each. With her support and encouragement, I continued forward.

Next, it was St. Margaret Mary's Church bazaar. I became a little craftier, putting googely eyes on my frogs. Don't laugh, they were a hit. The caterpillars were also a hit. Making $50.00 at this show really inspired me to do more.

Again, my friend Carole kept encouraging me. Did she know something I didn't? She suggested doing a mall show in Greece. That was really boring on Wednesday, until Friday, Saturday and Sunday. The price of each item did not include the time to make each one or the packaging, sales books and renting the space. Gosh, I sure had a lot to learn. Carole kept encouraging me. I need a name, because now I'm considered a business. My friend, Donna Taylor, who has since passed away, came up with the name in her kitchen. Donna was doing her own thing trying to lose weight, while making chocolate molds to sell for Easter and I was making figurines out of the clay. "A light bulb moment", Donna yells out, how about…………..

Adoughables By Carol!!!!!!

Yes, they are a type of dough. I had been making Bakers to hang on the wall. I even started using wooden plaques with an old-fashioned bride & groom glued on them. I kept thinking of all the things I wanted to create, like Charlie Chaplin, the Marx Brothers, Laurel & Hardy and Mae West. Time to go downtown to register my "name" and get a tax number. *Carole would say "now you are an artist". I'd say, "not yet".*

The Adoughbles Story

Everything Was by Trial and Error.

Each original design is handmade from bread dough (not edible of course) and duplicated by hand to give you an actual feeling of its originality. The Webster native began working in the dough medium as a hobby in 1973, a time when she says she had no artistic talent at all. "I had two young boys and make frogs ants, and worms out of baker's clay," she said. "They were big and clumpy," she says thinking back on her original pieces. Soon her repertoire was expanded to include caterpillars and Santa Clauses. She later began exhibiting in small arts and craft shows and church bazaars, but her perseverance didn't stop there.

"I'm obsessed with it," she said of her craft. "It's an all-consuming passion. I decided I had to make it a career." That all-consuming passion becomes evident as Graziano reveals the schedule she maintains as a full-time working mother.

After working a 9-to-5 job, Graziano would come home and spend hours in her basement workroom, sometimes until 2 or 3 a.m., laboring to complete a new addition to her Adoughable family. "It's been my escape," she said. "I find nothing more relaxing."

Beginning with the sandwich bread, Graziano breaks off the crusts and puts the remainder in a food processor to make fine bread crumbs – a step she used to do by hand while watching TV. She then adds glue until the dough is the right consistency.

From there, the actual creation may take hours to design because of the detail she puts into each one. And because she won't use molds, she makes each figurine's legs, followed by the body, and then head and hair, each part taking 24 hours to air dry.

The hair, she said, is done with a garlic press. "I spend countless hours on one figurine," Graziano said. Many of the ideas she gets for her Adoughables come her own memories as a little girl and things she used to do with her mother. She also gets ideas for poses, outfits, and facial expressions by watching little children, how they act and how they wear their hair.

"They are an extension of myself," Graziano said. "These kids become my kids, my babies." There are times Graziano will create a figure and not be able to part with it upon completion. "There is virtually no end to what can be created," she said.

Believe

At a garage sale I had, I was talking to this lovely young lady and her two daughters. She told me her Mothers' name was Millie. I only know one Millie that I have known for years. Millie and Jim had a beautiful son named Chad. Chad went to heaven much too soon and I had made an angel for him. I also made an angel for his sister. I never did finish an angel for his other sister named Lindsey. My gut feeling was that I was talking with Lindsey. I happened to have an angel sitting on my table, which I gave to her, now so many years later. The angel had "" Believe" written on it. Lindsey gasped, saying this word "Believe" is the center of her whole life. It was meant to be that she has this special angel after all these years. That was the hi-light of my day.

Adam's Story

Adam was a custom-made figurine.

Adam's mother called me asking if I could make a figurine from her favorite picture of her son. Adam was killed in a car accident. It's important to know that there was a shooting star out that night falling from the sky. The picture she sent me was of Adam at a younger age. This time I asked God to guide my hands. I wanted it to be special and Capture Adam as his mother remembers that day. I made a falling star on the top of his fishing pole. I received a beautiful letter from his Mom who was very pleased.

M & M's

One of my very first pins was a M & M pin.

Anybody can make a round circle, so mine had to be special. I actually took a bite out the M & M and then painted the bite to show the inside, and painted the "M" on top. I sealed each pin, so they would go through the washer and dryer at least one time. Then I thought I should send one to Mars Candy Co. hoping they would be interested. I received a letter from them saying I was infringing on their copyright and to please discontinue making them.

Howdy Doody

There was an ad in the newspaper that Howdy Doody, Buffalo Bob and Clarabelle were going to be at a local mall. "It's Howdy Doody Time" was a TV series from 1947-1960. He was a

marionette. Growing up at that time, it was a very popular show. Now that I was all grown up and doing my dough figurines not until 1973 through the present, I just had to go and see them at the mall.

I was making Howdy Doody pins.

I didn't know what to expect, meeting Buffalo Bob and his other side kick Clarabelle the clown.

I must admit I was just as excited as all those young kids waiting in a very long line. My turn to present my Howdy Doody pin. He was very gracious, smiling and asked how it was made and what inspired me. How well I remembered during his show he would yell out "What time is it?" We would yell back "It's Howdy Doody time." He seemed thrilled to hear my story.

The next day I got a phone call. He said this is Bob Smith. I said "Who?". This is Buffalo Bob from the Howdy Doody Show. He asked if he could order more of the pins. Of course, I replied. He told me he would send me a letter on how many and where to send them. I was very impressed

receiving his request on his official letter head paper. He had shown the pin to some of his friends.

Buffalo Bob Smith

4005 NORTHEAST 22nd AVENUE • COUNTRY CLUB DRIVE • FT. LAUDERDALE, FLORIDA 33308

May 6. 1989

Dear Carol,

It's been many moons since I last saw you in Rochester.

I still have one of my Howdy Doody Ahoughtobls left and get great comments on it.

Theight it be possible for you to make a few more for me? I shall be happy to pay you - or send a beautiful Howdy Doody watch to you. Please write to me at

BIG LAKE, PRINCETON. ME. 04668.

We plan to be there after May 16th.

Hugs
Bob

I also received a letter from Howdy Doody's grandmother. She said she was Buffalo Bob's sister. Enclosed was a hand embroidered hanky as a gift for me. She was thrilled and proud of the pin Bob had given her.

It now is in her hutch along with all her collection of Hummel figurines. Bob, I can call him that now, since I now know him on a personal basis, ordered even more pins.

ADOUGHABLES

Creativity comes in all forms, work, recreation and relationships. Unlocking your creativity, you create greater joy in your life and others!!

Glitter in My Pot Roast

I met Sandy and Dorothy at a mall show where I was exhibiting my "Adoughables". At the time, they were interested in my manger set. They asked if they could help me out someday with my inventory. We all became best of friends as they showed up at my house every single Thursday evening for 20+ years, despite snow storms, rain or hail.

One-day Sandy brought "Little Mary" with her. Little Mary and Sandy became my "Glitter Queens". When they left my house, they were totally covered from head to toe with glitter. They would cover all my angel wings with this beautiful diamond dust glitter that would sparkle, hanging from any Christmas tree with the true sparkle of "angel dust". Sandy

always brought donuts. We had the best group therapy once a week. Looking so forward to getting together was the happiest times. We laughed and giggled until our tummies hurt.

It's a rare occasion that a group of friends can really do some hard core laughing until happy tears were running down our cheeks so hard we all needed tissue. My last hour with Dorothy while she was in hospice, all we talked about was our Thursday nights together. Little Mary also grew her own wings and went to heaven laughing all the way. Now Sandy had become the only prestige Queen of Glitter.

I taught Dorothy how to make some dough flowers and gather them into beautiful miniature bouquets for my angels and dolls. Sandy also made hands on my angels, sometimes two left hands or two right hands. After seeing all these angels with two right hands, again we burst into hysterical laughter. I remember doing a signing of the duplicated dolls at one of my store sales.

I found one with two left hands and quickly put that one under the table. That made that doll truly rare. Imagine three grown women counting the inventory. We kept coming up with three different counts. We finally touched each figurine while we counted until we came up with the same number. Back to my Glitter Queen, Sandy. She called me to tell me that her wonderful and understanding husband, Jerry, said one morning getting out of bed, "what's this, glitter in our bed?" The best call from Sandy was, "there is glitter on my pot roast that I just took out of the oven.

Sandy and Dorothy helped at inside shows such as the three day show at the Rochester Museum and Science Center. One time we all bought the same light weight fall jacket from a vendor close by. It has been such a delight reminiscing all these times together. They still bring laughter.

I had more Queens in by basement helping me, "Bread Queens". Elaine and her daughter Michelle both of whom have flown away with their own developed wings to watch over us. The delightful story about them is, sometimes I would catch them taking a bite of the bread while they were taking the crust off some fresh bread. After they did it, we all did. Most of the time there was more crust leftover, so Elaine would take it home and make a bread casserole, Kugel. We all would have Kugel for dessert along with donuts.

 There also is a great friend named Cindy, who was a "Queen De-cruster". I would drop off the bread to her house and pick it up later, all de-crusted. Also, her wonderful husband, Matt, who fixed my terribly rusted 1976 Ford van. He secured all the holes in the van like the hole beneath my gas pedal and the roof. We are who we are from our memories, whether good or bad, we have grown while developing our own wings.

Craft Shows

My first big show was the Clothesline Art show held at the Memorial Art Gallery in Rochester, NY. I cannot forget all those shows that Sharon Kahler organized in her garage. All the vendors got a list of where to tape a flyer that Explained all about the big, big event at Sharon's address. I am in awe of this woman. She could organize a State Fair with no problem. Sharon went from garage shows, **Co-op shows**, 2 & 3 at a time, to renting out empty stores in a mall and then the Spring and Fall shows she organized at **Casa Larga Vineyards**. She even arranged a signing event for "Me" in my home town, Webster, NY. **I was signing my Limited Edition of the "Carol Ann Doll."** Sharon ordered a cake with a picture of me at about 5 years old in my hand-me-down dress and sausage curled hair on top of the cake. She took care of the advertising also. You can still check out

Sharon's' creations at **The Shops on West Ridge**. I just got off the phone with Sharon, asking if I could talk to her for a few minutes. She said sure, but was on her way to Myrtle Beach, and said she would call me right back. She is something, she did call right back. Sharon will always make time for everyone. She is still doing the show at Powers Market in Fairport, NY, on Palm Sunday every year. Back to the **Clothesline Art Show**. There I was, in my winter coat, no tent and its sprinkling. Everyone is setting up their booth.... not prepared....... still lots to learn. I did have a very large piece of see-through plastic to cover my inventory, but nothing to cover me. I have got to buy a tent.

Park Avenue Show usually has one day of rain, hail, wind or a thunder storm. I can't forget wind, rain and lightning that one day. Jilly & I were standing across from each other holding on to metal poles. I looked at her and cried out, "Do you realize it's lightning with a terrible wind and we are hanging on to metal poles?" We quick let go and started grabbing inventory to put as

much as we could under the table. Eventually I did buy a tent. I still ran into problems.

At the **Fairport Canal Days Show**, I forgot the hooks for the side panels of my tent. (I still haven't found them.) At the Corn Hill Show, I forgot the top of my tent. I did have time to go home and pick it up. At the **Art Museum Show**, it was 5 PM and the show had just ended. Everyone was tearing down their displays and packing their inventory, when the fire alarm went off, and we were told to leave the building. You just had to be there, unless you can envision a couple hundred artists outside, shivering cold and all holding their cash boxes, no

coats on. I met Sandy Bills and Dorothy Rosenbauer at the mall show. As a matter of fact, I met most of my best friends at a show. The rewards that you get out of doing a show are tremendous. Hearing, "I have to have that "with a smile and enthusiasm. When you win a ribbon, "Best of Show "or "Best in your Category" or even second place. It's such a rush and pushes you on to create more. That two-minute TV time, the newspaper article, may be a one liner or a full-page article is just so awesome.

My Jilly

I like to call her Jilly, but her name is Jill Kless. She had been collecting my figurines for some time. While showing my work at the Clothesline Art Show, Jilly came up to my booth asking if I needed some help. O golly, you bet I do.

She jumped right in. She took right over, gently packaging every item. It felt like she never left my side for 12 years. We shared some remarkable times at local shows and out-of-town shows.

Jilly became the cashier, receipt person, still very gently packaging, balancing all the receipts and inventory. Guess what I did? Talk, yes, I can talk, to potential customers with a tremendous amount of questions. She helped me type up my directions for all my **Continuing Education classes**. I talked, she typed. It wasn't as easy as you would think. We laughed through most of it. At shows, Jilly helped set up my tent and take it down at the end of the day, starting at 7 a.m. and finishing at 8 p.m. She helped set up inventory at the opening of a show and at the end of the show she was there gently packing up. Jilly could pack my car or that old rustic 1976 Ford van in such an organized fashion. I will be forever grateful to her.

On the Road Adventures

Usually, Corn Hill was the two hottest days of the year. Park Avenue usually had one day maybe rain and lightning or wind and maybe hail. We have some remarkable stories about out-of-town shows, like "on the road adventures."
Check it out, Jilly – *there is a horrendous black cloud coming right at us.* Sure enough, here it comes. A black, I'm going to call them a gang of 'BEES.' They flew behind us and all landed in a tree behind our tent. Now you must know we were petrified. Thank goodness, some gentlemen came to our rescue and sprayed the tree. They all left. We were left with still feeling petrified.

I had a large 1976 Ford van that was so rusted, a board had to be placed under my feet because it was rusted out. The whole van was pretty much rusted out, but... It took us, our inventory, our tent and tools to quite a few shows. Then there was the day coming home from a Batavia show and ran into a snowstorm, no a blizzard, on the Thruway. You couldn't see two feet in front of you. What else could go wrong? You guessed it. The van broke down. We were freezing and hungry. We finally got picked up by a tow truck that could only take us to the Thruway exit. Because there were two men in the tow truck, Jilly and I had to ride in the van while being towed. That was scary.

Because Jilly's house wasn't too far from the Thruway, they towed us to her house. Later, I called the auto service and was towed to my house, where it sat for a few days.

If you have ever been to the Clothesline Art Show at the Memorial Art Gallery, you know there are a few very small hills that could be very dangerous if you were all packed up and tired from a wonderful day leaving the gallery and having no brakes. I'm yelling *Jilly, we're going to hit that car! I have no brakes!* We did hit the car and, fortunately, the driver was very understanding and there was no damage. Oh, gosh, another tow?

Syracuse, raining, oh, so rainy day. The grounds were getting soft, then very muddy. I was still using my 1976 Ford rust mobile. We were all packed up and going home. Oh, no, we weren't. We were stuck in the mud. This is serious. There is a lot of mud flying from my tires trying to get some momentum. Yay, to our rescue again. Some gentlemen got behind the van and pushed. Oh, dear, they pushed, and the mud flew all over them, covered. All I could say is I'm so sorry, thank you, and bless you.

Just one more. We are all set up at **Letchworth State Park** for the Columbus Day weekend. Our first day was great, cold, but great. We covered our inventory and went back in the morning. I saw a vendor holding a mop cleaning off the frost INSIDE the roof of her tent. Not knowing why, I asked. She told me if you don't, the frost that builds up during the very cold evening will melt and rain on your inventory when the sun comes out.

I don't have a mop! I took a very long stick, taped lots of paper towels to it. By now I have become well prepared for just about anything. It took a while. OK, I'm ready for a sunny day.

Park Avenue Festival. A rainy day that turned into hail, big balls of hail. So hard this hail was coming down that it was breaking the pottery that was being displayed next to me. Trial and error again. I learned when there is a torrential rainstorm, store your inventory in see-through plastic boxes, not the cardboard ones.

Trial & Error…. Success

My biggest challenge with trial and error was when I made an "L" shaped mold from plaster. I made it for the body and legs of my dolls. The mold came out great. I placed colorful and different styles of dresses over each plaster mold. One week later counting the inventory…. oh my! I forgot the dough shrinks and the plaster does not. All those pretty dresses were now all cracked. Peeling the dough off was easy. I bought a miniature dress pattern and material. Cutting out the dresses, I then starched them and put them on each doll. I made a matching hat and purse for each doll. Success!

My Sunday line became a popular line. I also put doll hair under each hat. Finally, a trial and error ended in success.

"Something you will never forget
is how that someone made you feel"

… One of my favorite quotes from Maya Angelou

Special Friend Angel is Truly a Gift

10 Angels

...what could be better than having an angel by your side to make you smile, touch your soul, and bring you comfort. Each original design is handmade from bread dough (not edible of course) and duplicated by hand to give you an actual feeling of its originality.

Baby in Every Fold

My vision of this angel was a baby in every fold of her robe. She represents the innocence, love, joy, unconditional love; the beginning of

life. At that moment, there was much peace in heaven, but voices from Earth could already be heard. And the child in a hurry asked softly *"Oh, God, if I am about to leave now, please tell me my angel's name…"* … *"You will call your angel 'Mommy.'"*

Erica

"Erica, Will You Marry Me?"

I was asked if I could write these words on one of my angels holding a banner. Erica had been collecting my angels. Her fiancé thought that asking her in this way would be more personal. I replied with great enthusiasm that I would be honored to share in such a memorable occasion.

She said "Yes"

Mother/Daughter

That proud and happy feeling looking down at her daughter or my granddaughter holding her mom's hands with love and joy and pride, and in return the child looking up at mom also with love and admiration.

Mother/Son

Being cuddled in the arms of this angel with that sense of belonging.

Shoe-a-holic, Shop-a-holic, Choc-a-holic AND (Yes, I'm all of them. LOL)

P.S. Choc-a-holic Angel will be back she has gone off to Over Eaters Anonymous due to a little too much Chocolate, don't tell anyone.

Barefoot Angel

Angel with twins (barefoot). Line consists of angels, bare feet, and holding bouquets of flowers.

This angel pictured was a barefoot angel holding boy and girl twins. This a custom order from a mother to her daughter.

Speaking of bare feet, while in Aruba, we found a vacant beach. I ran down that beach, screaming as loud as I could "Free, I feel so free." To my dismay, I looked down at my bare feet loaded with black tar. We spent the afternoon cleaning my feet with nail polish remover.

Butterfly Angel

Because I started out making caterpillars that have turned into lovely butterflies, this angel became a great inspiration to create.

"We delight in the beauty of a butterfly, but rarely admit the changes it has gone through to achieve that beauty." Maya Angelou

9~11 Angel

Creating an angel with a tear flowing down her cheek with the American flag painted on her dress. I believe that says it all.

"Little Mary".

Our Little Mary who was our first Glitter Queen has grown her own wings. I am sure she has her paint brush loaded with glitter painting angel's wings. Maybe one of those shinning stars in the sky at night are one of Mary's painted wings.

My Sister

This angel is very dearest to me.

It was created from all the memories of my precious sister, Marsha. I called her Sis, she called me Sis. Passing out gifts at Christmas did get confusing; which Sis does this gift go to? I went to Nevada to care for her through the transition into hospice.

As difficult as it was for both of us, we were able to spend every holiday from November through February together. *e sure made every holiday special as always. I knew it would be the last.*

Our Mom always told us, whenever a heart-breaking tragedy occurs, down the

road there will be some comfort to follow. There was the huge gathering of so many of her friends celebrating her life. I was, and I still am always looking for signs that she is around. On the plane home, I carried her with me and there was a rainbow.

Walking into Wegmans, I heard her favorite song playing over the loudspeaker. I started my sister's angel, knowing how much she loved the outdoors being under the sun, moon and stars. This angel also went Nation-wide in her memory.

Honorary Angels

It was the "Support our Troops" angel that had a tremendous effect on my whole being. What I had to offer you, you in return are offering me to continue, keep going.

P.S. Breast Cancer Angel is out healing today, she will be back soon.

The Recipe Card Kneeded Angels

Out of the great mixing bowl of life came the Kneeded Angel's. Each Kneeded Angel is creatively kneaded, rolled and wrapped to become a one of a kind masterpiece. They are all handmade from a very special dough-like material. The originals, created by Carol Graziano, use the same technique, however are made with bread and glue. The Kneeded Angels are accompanied by an inspirational recipe card.

The recipe card says what is often difficult for one to put into words. As Carol always expresses with passion, "we need them, and they kneed you.........."

Wedding Cake Topper Stories

I love You, in sign language.

One venture that has been successful is her $375 **wedding-cake** figurines, which she designs to match the clothes, hair and jewelry that a couple plans to wear on their big day – even including a beaded flip-flop, body piercings and a kilt, not all on the same person.

The 2003 cake topper for Peter and Suzette Boulay of Pittsford includes Peter's wheelchair, the brace he wears on his left hand and the couple's wire-framed eyeglasses.

"We got tons of compliments on it," says Peter Boulay, "It looked just like us, says Suzette Boulay, "I felt it was well worth the money." They store their miniature selves under a glass dome in their family room.

The process of creating these detailed figures is a lengthy one, but one she refers to as a labor of love. Sitting in Graziano's home, you can see that she loves her work. A photo album of the bridal cake tops she has made through the years is among her works. The figurines bear a striking, uncanny resemblance to photos of the real brides and grooms. Graziano said that she spends hours creating them in likenesses of the couple, right down to the sequins on a dress and the flowers in a bouquet.

Whether it's a spit curl on the bride or a replica of the groom's favorite shows, the figurines sport fine details of their everyday lives as well. She points to little pink jogging shoes delicately dangling from a bridal figurine to illustrate her point. Each creation is take to heart, and Graziano goes to great lengths to make sure her Adoughables are true-to-life.

"I've even gone to florist to see what the bouquet looks like and to dress shops to see the back of bridal gown that you can't see in a photo," she added. She said many couples have brought their cake tops back after a few years to have her add a baby or two to round out the family – a request she fulfills willingly.

Each of Graziano's "Sunday Best" line – Maggie, Jillie, Rebecca, and Ebony – is different, from the dresses they wear to the bows in their hair.

The fine detailing includes everything from knuckles on fingers to folds in the dresses, and has resulted comparisons to Hummel figurines. The process of creating these detailed figures is a lengthy one, but one she refers to as a labor of love.

A photo album of the bridal cake tops she has made through the years is among her works. The figurines bear a striking, uncanny resemblance to photos of the real brides and grooms. Graziano said that she spends hours creating them in likenesses of the couple, right down to the sequins on a dress and the flowers in a bouquet.

Whether it's a spit curl on the bride or a replica of the groom's favorite shows, the figurines sport fine details of their everyday lives as well.

She points to little pink jogging shoes delicately dangling from a bridal figurine to illustrate her point. Each creation is take to heart, and Graziano goes to great lengths to make sure her Adoughables are true-to-life.

Custom-made Wedding Tops in the image of the Bride and Groom Wedding Cake Top Figurines as unique as you are. Wedding attire details featured in each figurine as seen in photographs provided.

Lightweight "treasures", a keepsake. Personal features: Hairstyle, hair color, your bouquets, mustache, glasses, etc. Your Wedding Cake Top can be further personalized to reflect your special interests, hobbies or profession.

Three Generations

29 years ago, I was working in an office with a young girl named Voirrey. She got engaged and wanted me to make her wedding cake topper. This would be my second one. I wanted it to be three dimensional. Perseverance again took over. I did it with much excitement. Voirrey and Christopher's topper opened a whole new experience for me. Finally, I created a lightweight base to set on a standard 5-inch base on the cake. Now I could advertise that my wedding cake toppers could be placed in a dome after the wedding. Two years ago, I made Voirrey and Christopher's son 's wedding topper, Tim and Mary. 2017 I had the privilege in making another son's wedding topper Cahal and Caitlyn. Their daughter, Garrison and Dean will be getting married in June 2018. I am so honored to share such a special day with this so special family. I pray that I will be able to create the toppers for my grandchildren.

One of my beautiful brides left her cake topper on her dining room table. Her Dog jumped on the table and literally ate the groom and left his feet imbedded in the base. The dog never touched the bride, thank goodness. I was able to reproduce the groom, so all was well.

This cake topper was for a 50th Anniversary. Unusual and fun to do. 50 years ago, this couple was dressed traditionally, bride in her gown and groom in his tuxedo. On their 50th anniversary the kids wanted Mom dressed in the tux and Dad dressed in Mom's wedding dress. You can imagine the second looks and laughter. Mom wanted to know why Dad had so much hair since he is now balding.

At this wedding, someone came up and ripped the head off the groom. No problem for me, I replaced the head, and all was well. When there is a discrepancy regarding how much hair should be on the groom. One picture shows a lot of hair and another picture, not so much. Time for me to call the bride. Her instructions were, make his hair in between. A bride and groom, under a tree with their initials carved into the tree inside a heart.

One time a bride brought back her topper because the elbow on her figurines became broken. I had her broken arm and it fit perfect, gluing it back on. She did break her arm at the same place. We laughed, saying maybe she was a voodoo doll.

Then there are the Mr. and Mrs. Donald Duck with the bride's dress on Mrs. Duck. Mrs. Duck in her original wedding dress, provided by her pictures, veil, crown and holding her bridal bouquet. Mr. Duck in his tux with trail, vest, top hat, gloves, and bow tie. Another great challenge since I have never done ducks for a cake topper.

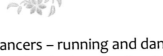

My ballroom dancers – running and dancing toward each other. They later thanked me for "making our wedding so memorable with your delightful dancing cake topper. It was a total hit." "It was an extra special touch that made our wedding celebration wonderful and joyful."

Another topper had the bride and groom with a canoe in front of them. In the canoe was their pet dog and an album reading "Our Wedding Day". **The canoe had "Sweet Dreams"** written on it with two oars and two golf balls.

Can't forget the "Love Is" couple. They were both in the entertainment business. Groom in his tux holding a guitar and the Bride in her dress with her keyboard. Written on the keyboard was "Love is Jennifer and Jason".

Another topper had the couple dressed in their **scuba gear.** The base was sand, and the couple were standing under a palm tree. Dressed in their diving tanks, the groom in flippers, with one foot up, his flipper read "Help".

This topper was a retired couple on the beach, with the base done with sand. The bride had a nurse's cap on her head and a bowling ball next to them.

The couple Peter and Suzette Boulay presented a big challenge for me since I have only been making figurines of bride and groom for Wedding Cake Toppers.

Peter's wheelchair and the brace he wears on his left hand had to be perfect. Finally completing Peter's wheelchair, now how do I get Peter in it? I finally did manage to do that with much pride. They told me they got tons of compliments at the wedding. "They looked just like us".

Klassic Kringles

Mr. and Mrs. Clause. This was a very big challenge for me. It is difficult to put two figurines together and hope, 'I do mean hope", they dry together.

"Wa la, it worked." My vision of these figurines was having Mrs. Clause making cookies for Santa before his so very long trip on Christmas Eve. For each Santa, I had to make an ornament of the same.   There were eleven Santa's in total along with eleven ornaments of each. Some of the larger Santa, which were 8 inches in height, had music inside of them.

Santa with a large leather belt that had bells all around played, you guessed it, "Jingle Bells".

Recipe card enclosed with Kneeded Angel

"Season of Joy"
 2 cups Holiday Cheer
 ¾ cup Good Spirit
1 tbl. Sugarplums
Combine holiday cheer and good spirit to get a warm fuzzy Christmas feeling. Garnish with sugarplums and serve with hot chocolate by a warm crackling fire. **Remember – You Knead them, and they Kneed you!**

Christmas Angel

It seems I become more creative during the Christmas season. To me, it means a coming together, a celebration with family &friends. There is joy in the air, peace and hope for the future.

My angel placing a star at the top of the Christmas tree covered in red bows will soon be bursting with bright colored lights. She is one of my most favorite angels. This is the time of the year I introduce my limited-edition angel that is signed, dated and numbered. I have a following that I have the opportunity to see for the past 17 years. I started my limited-edition angel in 1984 from a customer who suggested I do every year.

I haven't been doing shows for a few years now and every year I say this will be the last one. Then, the season starts. I get excited and someone calls and asks if this year will be the last, I'm inspired and cannot say no. I guess I will continue until I can't physically carry on. I'm hoping that I will be able to make my granddaughter and grandson's wedding cake toppers.

Nativity Set

My nativity set consisted of Baby Jesus, Mary, Joseph and two lambs. I used the crust for their outer robes, depending on my mood at the time, and the white part of the bread for their inner robes, or vice versa. I wanted them to be very natural and simple. Baby Jesus has the swaddling around him from the white part of the bread. The lambs do have white paint mixed into the dough. I was speaking to my Lord, asking him to guide my hands and to help me to create my vision of peace and serenity.

It Is Not a Dream Anymore!

My dream of seeing my work displayed in a gift shop has come true! It all started when I was displaying my work at the Park Avenue Festival in Rochester, NY, August 3, 2000 at 3:00 p.m. Pavilion Gift Company, located in Bergen, NY approached me. (We had a meeting the following week and my life has become a whirlwind of creativity, excitement, joy, and emotional bliss ever since.) They asked me if I could create 22 new designs of angels by October. My answer, "You Bet I Can." After all, I have been making angels for many years. Twenty-four angel designs and my 11-piece Nativity set hit the gift show market across the country in January 2002.

In December, I saw the entire finished product on display at their showroom. I asked if I could be alone with them for a moment. The tears trickling down my face, my heart pounding with excitement, oh, my, it is really happening, it is not a dream. I had to call my sons, Jamie and Patrick, and my friends to share this moment of my life. Of course, no one was home, so I just left a very emotional message. I will never forget that special moment, along with many more to come.

"The Kneeded Angels" have arrived. As most of you know, all my originals are made by hand and made from white glue and bread and kneaded to a very smooth clay-like material. They are sent to the Orient for reproduction. Even in the Orient, they are being made by hand. Again, no two pieces the same. They are being made from a soft resin.

I would like to personally thank each and every one of you for all the support through the years. A special thank-you to my fellow crafters! Thank you to Jill, Carole, Sharon, Sandy, Dorothy, and Jane. Gosh, I feel like I have won an Oscar. I have! Together with Pavilion Gift Company, we are a great team.

Reward for Perveance
Signing in England

When Pavilion Gift Company told me, I was going to England to do a show, I realized my dreams are for sure becoming bigger than I ever expected. Coming into the showroom there were 20-foot silk screens of my angels, hanging from the high ceilings. All of them just took my breath away. I was hoping my Mom; my Dad and my Sis were watching. I had never been out of the country other than Canada. I never felt alone, because I met so many beautiful people so willing to help me from the time I arrived at the airport, to when I had to leave. It was truly an experience trying to understand so many accents of the English language and driving on the opposite side of the road. I loved and cherished every second. I have never had a problem talking about my work. I was so eager to explain how the designs of all the figurines were made. We all worked very hard at the so very big showroom and we played very hard in the evenings. At every signing in different states, I swear by the end of an evening my feet felt like I was walking on swollen balloons. These wholesale shows were all hustle and bustle every minute. Waiting for the signing to begin and being told the line was down this huge hallway and around the corner. When asked if I wanted to take a break, I would say, "Oh no", I've waited all my life to be here never dreaming it would be this big or this exciting. The heartfelt stories I was hearing from people waiting for me, yes, "Me" to sign a figurine.

I saw a silver heart that read, "I said a prayer for you today." I bought that heart and still have it today. That heart inspired me to do a whole new line of angels, like "Follow your dreams", "Our Friendship is a Gift" and more.

Highland Hospital gift shop signing: my good friend, David, set me up in his gift shop. If you see David, ask him what we call each other. I met up with a neighbor I haven't seen in at least ten years. Her daughter and my son were playmates when they were young. Reminiscing is so enjoyable.

Saint Ann's gift shop signing: They also carried my figurines and it turned out to be one of my busiest signings. I'm sure many of you can remember Lock, Stock and Barrel. I would go in that store and dream of having my work being there someday. I had my faith wrapped around that dream, because it came true.

Hallmark Store signings where the advertising and the set up were right at the front entrance of each store. There were many more signings.

It has been a true Cinderella story.
From ants, worms and caterpillars to beautiful butterflies,
the googely-eyed frogs didn't turn into a handsome prince,
but I turned into a real Cinderella.

Where Are My Angels Now?

At a job review, as I was walking thru the office, I saw three of my angels sitting on the desks of some of the employees. This really put a smile on my face.

Parking my car in North Carolina, going to get souvenirs, I parked
next to a car with one of my angels mounted on the dashboard. I
waited for the person to come out of the store to tell him that the angel was created by me.

Walking into an angel shop in Florida, I noticed a woman holding two of my angels. I asked her if she would like me to sign them, because they were my creations. She smiled, I smiled and with such joy I signed them.

In a casino and going to cash in my winnings, there was one of my angels sitting on a shelf.

We, all of us are angels walking around with invisible little stubs on our backs that are slowly developing into full blown angel wings someday.

eBay and various collector websites.

Success

I had the fortunate experience of meeting someone on Facebook who told me her story of wanting to turn her fantasy into reality. We became friends on Messenger. I told her of my experience with perseverance meeting up with opportunity and I was writing a book.

Wrapping your dreams and goals in faith, and they will explode beyond your dreams.

Today, I have just heard that has happened. A video and television program has become her dream. I can't tell you the joy and excitement I feel for her.

I remember while writing my book, and almost finished, if I could even encourage one person not to give up that "gut feeling, that they have something to offer,"
I have succeeded.

Another story that must be written.

Most Asked Questions

Are these ceramics?

No. They're made of "glue dough" – Elmer's glue and sliced sandwich bread. I USE OVER 1300 LOAVES OF BREAD AND 60 GALLONS OF GLUE IN ONE YEAR.

Is this your own formula?

No. It was developed years ago to make miniatures, but I experimented until I found the more advanced techniques I use today. FORMULA: 1 Tbsp. glue and 1 slice de-crusted bread.

Are they baked?

No. They are air-dried. They need no sealer.

How do I care for them?

Just dust with a soft brush. Store in tissue in a dry place.

What kind of paint to you use?

Water colors, acrylics, food coloring – even house paint works.

Do you use molds?

No. Each head, arm, leg, etc. is made by hand.

How do you make the hair?

A garlic press and a toothpick.

How long does it take to make one?

The design of the first one may take hours. After that, it depends on the size of item, the amount of detail and the drying time between stages.

How long have you been doing this?

I began working in the dough medium as a hobby in 1973 and started my business in 1975. Over the years, I have developed my own specialized techniques and my own style, which continues to evolve.

When my schedule permits, I enjoy doing presentations on dough art at group events. I prefer to make pieces individually, since mass production takes away from my creativity. **There is virtually no end to what can be created – from pins to custom-made wedding cake tops – and more!**

Carol Ann Doll

In honor of my 20th Anniversary of Adoughables by Carol, I introduced my Carol Ann Doll.

Yes, that is a doll of me as a five-year-old child. Oh, how my mother took such pride in creating those beautiful sausage curls in my hair. My dress was a hand-me-down from cousin to cousin. I made a limited edition of 50 dolls, all originals, signed, dated and numbered.

I had a caterpillar in one hand. This was to represent the transition into a beautiful butterfly.

A friend, Sharon Kahler, set up a signing in a flower shop in the village of Webster, where I grew up. Leave it to Sharon, to have a special cake made with a picture of me at five years old. It turned out to be a remarkable success and was covered by the local newspaper with a beautiful article being published.

Out of the great mixing bowl of life.

Carol Graziano uniquely designed each Angel using her own special recipe.

Recipe for: The Kneeded Angels
1 Slice white bread
1 tbl. white glue
Knead bread & glue into dough using a large bowl.
Must Knead bread until it feels angel smooth.
Measure 1 tablespoon each of Inspiration, Love, Hope & Faith.
Combine with dough and add 2 parts Friendship and Prayer.
Knead once more while smiling.
Hold them up, look into their eyes and let them inspire you.

The Most Beautiful People

They have known suffering, struggle, loss, and have found their way out of the depths. These persons have an appreciation, a sensitivity, and an understanding of life that fills them with compassion, gentleness, and a deep loving concern.

Celebration, our 55th reunion

Beautiful people don't just happen. My classmates are beautiful people. We are the last to graduate from Webster Central High School fifty-five years ago, in 1962.

There is an open invitation to join our classmates for breakfast every Saturday at 9:00 AM at the Nutcracker Restaurant. There will always be at least ten or more at the restaurant. Around the holidays there are always more joining us.

Our most recent celebration, our 55th reunion, we chartered a school bus which back in the day, we all rode except for one. Being that I am a school bus monitor, I put on my bright yellow vest and announced the rules on the bus; keep your hands to yourself, legs out of the aisles, no standing while the bus is moving and no cussing. We took a memory tour downtown Main Street for the out-of-towners, to see all the changes to our city. Next stop, our good ole' Alma Mater, Webster High School. This building was built in the shape of a "W". At the end of our tour, we returned to lunch, served on picnic tables with potted plants, later given away as door prizes.

In the evening, we had a lovely catered dinner with all the trimmings. There were glass center pieces with candles and fresh flowers from the garden of one of our classmates. Many pictures of past reunions were laid out on a table for all of us to reminisce. We also had a table overflowing with donations, door prizes, and a raffle drawing. There was more the following morning. The Nutcracker Restaurant brought in toasted bagels with all the spreads, and large filled coffee urns. This accompanied fresh fruits, Danishes, and muffins. Good bye you most beautiful people.

No need for Ensure or energy boosters. I get my weekly strength from these people. Everything is right here; group therapy, innovative ideas for physical therapy, the latest in new meds, lots of support, and best of all, lots of hugs. Don't laugh, hopefully you too will become a beautiful person in your years to come. "Beautiful people do not just happen!"

Artistic Profile

the creator of Kneeded Angels™
Rochester artist
Carol Graziano

What do you get when you mix imagination, perseverance, sandwich bread, and Elmer's Glue? A hobby-turned business for Irondequoit's Carol Graziano.

Carol with her creativity, (Rochester, NY Artist) Carol A. Graziano shares her long-time dream of being able to inspire others as she has been inspired by family, friends and her own life's experiences. Following a recipe for a Christmas craft, back in 1973, has now become a recipe for a life's work. With Carol's mom's inspiration and seeing the amusement in the eyes of her two young sons, from the frogs, ants and worms first created, developed a discovery of a gift that Carol can now share with the world. 1500 loaves of sliced sandwich bread, mixed with gallons of glue each year – then kneaded to form a dough, have become creations to warm your heart and make you smile.

Acknowledgments

Thank you to all who supported me in my business endeavors, from the very first Adoughable to my continued craft in angels and wedding cake toppers.

Thank you especially to my Webster Breakfast club, for being my cheer leaders, and comrades through the years. And they are many.

A special, thank you to everyone, for encouraging the publishing of this book. To Helen and Jilly for their typing and correcting my manuscript. To Sandy, Barb, Jane and Dorothy. "The Glitter and De crusting Queens,". for the of the Pavilion Gift Company. Thank you to my publisher for believing in me.

By Special request

Our Healer Angel

Breast Cancer No More Angel

Made in the USA
Middletown, DE
08 January 2023

21681232R00033